(The TREMENDOUS POWER OF PC

Copyright © 2009 by (Gayle Kurtzer M

Disclaimer

responsibility of the reader. For information that applies to specific individual circumstances with regard to the anger management it is advisable to consult an attorney at law or a duly qualified psychologist who has specialized in the field of relationship studies and anger management.

The author and publisher of this positivity guide have made their best efforts to ensure that the information present in this book is both accurate and up-to-date as well as factual, however, they make no warranties (implied or otherwise) as to the accuracy or completeness of the contents herein and cannot be held responsible for any omissions, errors, or (out) dated material.

The information given in this guide book may not be suitable for every individual player and/or company or organization that is interested in creative a positive environment and as such it is advised that people implementing the guidelines present in this book in their day to day dealings with people both at the personal and professional levels (in the case of the owners of a company as well as its employees) should do so, purely at their own discretion.

The publisher and author assume no responsibility whatsoever, for any outcome (including litigation) resulting from the application of the information found in this book, either through following these guidelines or formulating policies based on the same.

Neither the publisher nor author shall, in any way be held liable for any damages including but not limited to special, incidental, consequential, or other forms of damage.

About the author

Introducing ......

Gayle Kurtzer-Meyers is a licensed community association manager for HOA properties in S. Florida. She has in excess of 20 years in property management including a tax credit senior living property. Her day to day experiences serving as a liaison between residents, board members and executive owners has cultivated her natural inclination to accentuate the positive in order to diminish the negative in situations.

Gayle has scored in the top 1% of standard I.Q. tests and has won multiple awards for her various talents.

She fuels her positive energy by participating in charity marathons and hobbies of art and outdoor life.
Gayle's caring of others with positive energy is infectious and she hopes that this book will enhance your mind set to use positive words to enlighten your life and those in your sphere of influence.

Contents

Contents

Disclaimer 2

About the author   4

o   Introduction   8

o   The neurological benefits of positive words   9

o   The social advantages of using positivity   10

o   Using positive words in day to day interactions   10

o   Problems can easily become situations 11

o   'Always' and 'never' can be switched for 'often'   11

o   'Should have' viz-a-viz 'could have'   12

o   'Bad 'is bad and it is 'unwise' not to see that   12

o   'Faults' can and indeed should become 'differences'   12

o   The computer virus example   13

o   Always think positive before reacting to situations   14

o   The bank cashier example   14

o   Understand negative circumstances   15

o   It is imperative that you accept a given situation   16

o   Train your mind to be really positive 17

o   Surround yourself with positive people   17

o   Use the power of your own mind   18

o   A 'mistake' is almost always a valuable 'lesson'   18

o   Have high standards when it comes to spoken words 18

o   Respect begets respect 19

o   Set a certain threshold level of tolerance   20

o   Learning to keep your temper in check   21

o   The hormonal issues   21

o   Your body will tell you when you are really angry!   21

o   Suppressed anger is rather like a volcano   22

o   Your anger is actually trying to tell you something   22

o   Always learn to control your reactions22

o   What if your childhood is still making you angry?   23

o   Reactivity can easily be destructive   23

o   Being self-aware and mindful 24

o   How to Move Forward24

o   Positive language at work   26

o   The ubiquitous 'Naysayer'   26

o   Example one   27

o   How positive words can help here   27

o   Example two   27

o   Different types of Negative & Positive words   29

o   Negative terminology and its impact   29

o   Positive words and phrases and how they work   30

o   Some of the more common negative language, 30

o   Various expressions that suggest carelessness 30

o   Phrases thatsuggest that the recipient is lying 31

o   Any expressions that seem to cast aspersions   31

o   Different types of highly demanding phrases   31

o   Unduly sarcastic or patronizing phrases   31

o   Learning how to utilize positive phrases   32

o   Informal exercise   32

o   Speaking positively at work 34

o   Changing your habits 34

o   "I'm sorry…" 36

o   If only…"   36

o   Using the Tremendous Power of Positive language   38

o   Children Are Automatically Empowered   38

o   Positive Words Will Tell A Child What They Can Do 38

o   Example   38

o   Step 1: Identify all The Negative Terms   39

o   Step 2: Learn Some Positive Phases   40

o   Step 3: Always Set the Appropriate Boundaries   40

o   Step 4: Evolve Your Positive Language   41

o   Conclusion   42

Introduction

Using positive words cannot only change an otherwise negative situation into a positive one but in the long run, it can also be pretty effective in terms of changing the very structure of your mind.

"A single word has the power to influence the expression of genes that regulate physical and emotional stress."

Mark Robert Waldman in Words Can Change Your Brain

The neurological benefits of positive words

As a matter of fact, whenever we use certain really positive words such as "love", "peace" and "kindness", we are actually getting ready to be in a position to modify our brain functions through the simple expedient of increasing highly cognitive reasoning, as well as strengthening the critical areas of our frontal lobes. As a matter of fact, using certain positive words far more often than their negative counterparts can also easily activate the prime motivational centers of our brain, thereby propelling them towards really positive actions.

On the opposite end of the spectrum, we have clear-cut evidence that using negative words and their underlying connotations can effectively prevent certain neurochemicals (that exist in our neural pathways) from being produced. This, in turn, will end up contributing significantly to overall stress management.

So, in other words, whenever we allow any sort of negative words and concepts to creep into our thought processes, we are in effect, also increasing the actual, real-worldactivity in our brain's primordial fear center (the amygdala) and thus contributing to an increase in stress producing hormones that essentially flood our system. These neurotransmitters and hormones essentially interrupt the logic and reasoning processes of the human brain and thereby inhibit normal functionality, to a great degree.

o The social advantages of using positivity

The seminal importance of positivity in both our collective as well as our personal lives can never be overemphasized. Just pause and reflect upon it.How often does a person actually even think about the meanings of the words that he or she uses every day? By and large, we all do the same thing, and that is to just utter the words that somehow seem to flow quite naturally from our mouths. Unfortunately, some of the words that we quite commonly use might actually end up having a profoundly negative influence on the people around us, especially those people who care a lot about us and vice versa. Here, it is quite possible that this can create a really negative impression of the kind that will mar and damage a relationship with the very people that you really want to be on good terms with.

o Using positive words in day to day interactions

Of course, it does not always have to be this way at all. Let us take a look at some places where there might be an off chance that you will end up running into some sort of trouble by inadvertently using negative words when that was the very last thing that you had in mind. It does not have to be a serious conversation, per se. On the contrary, it can be anything as seemingly innocuous as leaving a message on your telephone answering machine, or talking with your favorite colleague at work,chatting with a neighbor, going to a parent-teachermeeting or any day to day interaction with your family and friends.

Let us see for ourselves how we can change the negativity around us by using multiple positive terms in order to create a more wholesome environment. In fact, if you were to get rid of a few negative terms and replace them with positive ones, you will be able to make a really positive change in your whole life. A change that will be reflected amongst your family and friends as well as any other people that you interact with, on a more or less regular basis.

o Problems can easily become situations

Let us take a fairly common negative statement and see how we can work our way around it till it sounds more positive and therefore easily doable as well.

"I have a problem at work." Now simply swap this statement with the farmore positive one, "I have a tough situation at work."

Here, the term 'problem' may ostensibly seem as if you stuck to in it and can't seem to get out of it, at all. Due to the seemingly intractable nature of this issue, it ends up weighing pretty heavily on your shoulders.

Now substituting the term, 'problem' with the comparatively more balanced 'situation', the latter term, on the other hand, can easily make it seem not just temporary but also easily solvable, as well. This is due to the fact that it has a considerably lighter feel to it, and as such it will not be able to cause all that much anxiety.

Always' and 'never' can be switched for 'often' and 'seldom'

It is quite possible to switch absolutes such as 'never' and 'always' with words that are less etched in stone, so to speak. Words such as 'seldom and often create a more ambiguous picture and thereby give you room to maneuver, even in tight spots.

o 'Should have' viz-a-viz could have': Know the difference

Various words such as "should have" may safely be converted to 'could have'. This means that the element of 'wishful 'thinking or regret has been taken away. When you use 'could' in lieu of 'would' what you are saying, in essence, is that the circumstances were not conducive to the right outcome. However, it was not really your fault, the outcome 'could have' swung either way. Here, when you use "should have" you are in essence accepting that everything was your own fault and you 'should' have done something entirely different. This way the onus of the blame lands squarely on your shoulders and you end up wallowing in grief and misery. The best way to dispel such unneeded negativity is to simply use positive or neutral terms and thereby ensure that you do not end up becoming guilty for anything that was not your fault, in the first place.

o 'Bad 'is bad and it is 'unwise' not to see that

As far as negative words go, 'bad' is as well, as 'bad' as it can get. Using this term means that the negative connotations attached to it also go for a ride, as well. Regardless of how you may look at it, you cannot safely use this word while maintaining a certain level of positivity, to go with it. Here, the term 'bad' can be safely switched to 'unwise' or some other less negative term.

o Faults' can and indeed should become 'differences'

When you go right ahead and tell a person that he is essentially at fault, then there is no way whatsoever, that he would be positive about it. Human beings are just not wired to think like that. We will become angry and defensive when someone tells us it's all 'our fault.' In "How to Win Friends and Influence People" Dale Carnegie had time and again emphasized that people cannot handle being called out for their faults at all. On the contrary, they will go out of their way to prove that you are wrong, and thereby end up unleashing a veritable firestorm of negativity in the bargain.

But if you were to think along the lines of swapping the term 'fault' with the term 'differences', then, of course, there will be an entirely new and comparatively more positive paradigm that will come into existence. Here, we use the term very 'differently' to say the least. Let us try and make the concept clearer with an example.

o   The computer virus example

A person unwittingly allows a terrible virus to enter a company's main servers. The virus locks away all the data present therein and refuses to let it go if a ransom amount is not paid. Here, the person who had unwittingly allowed it in can be taken to task by the company management who will blame him for his fault. However, that will only make him bitter and resentful. If his line manager were to counsel him to take more precautions by doing things a bit 'differently,' such as using an anti-virus scan check before opening unfamiliar attachments, then the said employee would see the error of his ways, without indulging in any negativity, in this regard. This way, the data will become secure and a valuable employee will also retain his overall productivity.

Always think positive before reacting to situations

"Keep your face to the sunshine, and you cannot see a shadow"

Helen Keller

It is pertinent to note that any individual or personality that essentially 'flies off the handle' (so to speak) with negative reactions usually has the potential to cause unintentional hurt to not only those that they are directing their emotions too but also the other individuals that are in the same environment and hear the wrath of the toxic behavior. Thus, if one unselfishly takes a moment to think of the positive aspects of a situation or person, the entire dynamics can be altered to result in a comparatively more positive outcome. Let us take a look at the following example:

o The bank cashier example

You go to a bank to cash a check a few minutes before closing time. The harried cashier has to cope with a long line of disgruntled customers and he is already frazzled as it is and yelling at the customers for not signing their checks properly. As you reach the counter, he looks at you with ill-concealed anger, but before he says a single word, you look him in the eye and compliment him on his hairstyle and how his full head of hair makes him look a couple of decades younger. Thoroughly disarmed, he breaks out in a heartwarming smile that makes both you and the cashierfeel completely at ease. When he goes back home, you can bet that he would be walking on air. Your quick and positive thinking had in effect, staved off what could have been a really negative situation into an otherwise really positive one.

However, this is but one example. In order to make it all work properly for you, it is important that you should try and make such positivity a part of your daily life. Let us take a quick look at how you too can try to stay positive in a negative situation.

o   Understand that negative circumstances are as much a part of your life as positive ones

First and foremost, it is very important that you understand the basic fact that just about everyone around, has to essentially go through at least some sort of adverse situation in his or her collective life. As a matter of fact, various adverse conditions generally make up a fairly large part of our life as they basically teach us exactly how to deal with different negative circumstances. Here, you will do well to remember that when you believe that you truly are on the right track, then it is an almost axiomatic assumption that you will need to face considerably more adverse situations than ever before. But if you see them as just a test, as well as a stepping stone for your success, you can come out on top, easily enough.

"You cannot have a positive life and a negative mind"

Joyce Meyer

In a nutshell, this means that being positive even during some of the greatest tragedies of life is essential. If you were to overcome the urge to say something wrong at the wrong moment then not only will your restraint allow you to be really happy in life, but at the same time it will also offer you awesome strength to be able to deal with just about any situation with a smile on your lips and a song in your heart. Following are a few pointers that can help you 'think before you leap' in any adverse situation:

o It is imperative that you accept a given situation and find a solution

Always remember "to err is human, to forgive divine." This means that people can and will make mistakes in each and every walk of life. And you are certainly no exception to this rule either. This is why there, is no point in worrying about it, a bit too much for comfort. And on top of that, to 'shoot your mouth' when others make the same mistakes. As a matter of fact, once you realize that you have made a mistake, it is high time that you learn to accept it and afterward, also learn to take all those steps that are deemed necessary to sort out the mess.

However, learning to 'bad mouth' at others will not only make them extremely defensive but at the same time they will resent you for your harsh words and bid their time till you make a mistake and end up in the same situation. Once, you do so, they pay you back in the same harsh coin, it will become a vicious cycle with no end in sight.

Yes, it is difficult to not lash out when you are angry and frustrated, but you can change, as and when required. Sometimes, the world will be in your favor, sometimes not, since change is an ever-evolving concept. This is why, no matter what, you have to learn to accept the situation as it is, without losing your temper and saying cruel and unkind things. The best way is to simply use positive words in order to mold the situation to your preference.

"Change your words and you will change your thinking and that, in turn, will change your actions"

Train your mind to be really positive

Nothing good or bad ever really happens. It is just our way of looking at it. In fact, it is the way we perceive the world around us that either makes it right or wrong for us. When you effectively make up your mind to treat every negative word, barb, andsituation as an object lesson to learn in life, you will in effect, be able to have a really positive outcome towards life in general, especially with reference to the power of the spoken word, and its ability to impact the people around you.

o   Surround yourself with positive people

The oft-repeated adage "A man is known by the company he keeps' is as fresh today as it was when it was first coined. As a matter of fact, this is the ultimate influencer of both individual character as well as the power of positive thought, and by extension, positive words as well. If you are always surrounded by negative people who speak only to deride and degrade their fellow human beings, then, of course, you too will be affected by their negativity and eventually end up following their way of thinking. Ultimately, they will be able to exert influence on not just your words alone, but also your thinking as well as your very character.

Conversely, when you start hanging out with positive people more often, then their positivity will also easily flow right into your soul. And once you have achieved a certain level of equilibrium with reference to your positive thoughts and words (not to mention actions) then that is where you will stay, and vice versa. If you really want to stay positive in life, then it is imperative that you try and avoid naysayers at all cost, so that you will always be surrounded in an aura of peace, serenity, and positivity.

o   Use the power of your own mind

You need to use not just your words, but your mind very mind in such a way that all the stress that you feel seeps out and you are only filled to the brim, with new positive thoughts and words.

Once you have a positive mind, then it is almost inevitable that positive words will flow through, and you will be able to turn even otherwise really negative circumstances, into highly positive ones.

"Positive anything is better than negative nothing"

Elbert Hubbard

A 'mistake' is almost always a valuable 'lesson'

When we chide others for making a mistake, we are making them bristle and they are on their guard, not so much to refrain from repeating the same mistakes, but rather to ensure that they have an adequate excuse whenever they make the same mistake. It cannot be stressed enough; exactly how important it is to make good and ensure that such erstwhile 'mistakes' are kept to a bare minimum. There are certain ways you can learn to ensure that the spoken word is not a mistake but a valuable lesson that you can easily utilize to the best of your abilities. Let us see how:

o   Have high standards when it comes to spoken words or at least some sort of standard

When things go wrong, it is all too easy to slip into gutter language and start cussing the people (as well as the world) around us. This is why it is very important to have high standards as far as your speech is concerned. Here the term 'self-respect' comes to mind. That is the higher your self-respect, the lesser will be the utilization of negative and just plain wrong terminology. If your spoken speech shows manners and elegance, then the people around you would be forced to raise the bar as well and before you know it, everyone would be refined and positive. And this does not have to be relegated to spoken speech alone. Rather you can utilize this principle on the basis of written text as well as each and every action of your life. This way, you will be able to create a wonderful example that everyone would love to emulate.

o Respect begets respect

If you respect others, they will respect you as well. If you are respectful towards your elders but talk to your juniors using negative speech and the kind of terminology that leaves them feeling bitter and vindictive, you are not doing yourself a favor. (To say the least.)

This is why you should not merely respect your elders, your bosses and your teachers alone. No, respect should always be part and parcel of your life. In other words, you have to respect 'everybody'. Not just your friends, family and coworkers.

When you start chewing out people who are not in a position to retaliate in any way, you will be abusing your power. On top of that, you have no idea what any person is actually going through or for that matter, what kind of background they are coming from. This is why everyone in the world is truly deserving of a basic and fundamental level of respect. Yes, it is not as easy as it sounds. Driving in a crowded city can, for example, often bring out the worst in us and we let the veneer of tolerance slip, which generally rests so uneasily on our visages.

However, this certainly does not mean that we have the inherent, god gifted right to be mean to people that we believe we will never be able to see again. Yes, it is easy to fall into the trap of our own anger and start screaming at the top of our lungs when someone jumps a red signal. But just stop and consider the fact that he is not likely to hear you, but unfortunately, the other occupants in your car might be made to listen to a sample of your highly negative and colorful vocabulary. This will demean you in their eyes. Especially because what has been said cannot really be unsaid. By ensuring the principle of "respecting everyone", you can easily make sure that you do not fall into this trap at all.

o Set a certain threshold level of tolerance

Being patient is all well and good, but let us face it, we are not Gautama Buddha. So, keeping your temper in check is all well and good, but there will come a time when the dam will break and the more you have kept a lid on it, the worse the resultant explosion will be. This is why it is very important that you have a certain limit when it comes to deciding just how far you can go before you start lashing out in a frenzy.

You have to make sure that your threshold limit is set well before the 'screaming and raving phase.' That is long before you start losing your temper. Under the circumstances, when you realize that speaking your mind and its positive thoughts are not going to do you any favors and will only invite even more very public opprobrium, it is important that you go right ahead and walk away from what is almost certainly a really annoying situation.

This holds true for your day to day life as well. Do not stick to a job simply because you are being paid to do something that you do not really like. This will increase your frustration levels and you will ultimately end up taking it out on your friends and colleagues.

Learning to keep your temper in check

In the heat of the moment, we sometimes end up saying and doing things that we should have avoided. In hindsight, we realize the folly of our errors and understand that it was basically a really(really) bad decision. However, words once said, can never really be unsaid, and that is precisely why we have to make the most of our mistakes and our follies by trying to control the damage. Here, the adage "an ounce of prevention is worth a pound of cure" comes to mind chiefly because it is as fresh and relevant today as it was when it was coined for the very first time. Let us see why it is so important to keep your temper in check all the time:

o   The hormonal issues

You should always aspire to control your temper because multiple stress hormones automatically flood your whole body as well as your mind when you are very angry. They effectively shut down the rational part of your brain. Without the veneer of sense and sensibility to aid your decision-making process, you can revert to a more primitive self— one that is driven by adrenaline and testosterone. Here the chances are that you are effectively stuck on autopilot when you do what you do. And only later, once the hormonal flush is over, do you realize the enormity of that you have done. But of course, by that time, it is way too late, and you cannot turn back the clock and unsay the harshness to which your loved ones have been exposed. However, wounds can heal, even if it takes them a long time to do so. And the good news is that you can easily create the kind of circumstances deep within you that will help you   control your temper to a great extent. Let us see how:

o   Your body will tell you when you are really angry!

Anger develops extremely rapidly. In fact, it develops so quickly and intensely that it is extraordinarily hard to realize exactly how angry you are really feeling, and this happens long before you get a chance to react. However, once you have learnt to recognize exactly what your anger does to your own body, such as making your face really hot or creating a lot of pressure in and around your neck, then you will be able to create the required space between the trigger that causes you to become angry and your reaction to that trigger.

o   Suppressed anger is rather like a volcano

Anger can not only make others really uncomfortable but can frighten them. Sometimes this is why people bottle up their negative emotions. So that they would not say the wrong thing in the heat of the moment. Unfortunately, that is exactly what they end up doing in the first place. The main problem with all this suppression, though, is that it ends up creating a veritable mountain of explosive feelings that more often than not, end up eventually erupting in some very harmful ways. These include physical illness, mental depression, self-destructive behaviors, etc.

o   Your anger is actually trying to tell you something

Anger is basically your brain's way of telling you that something is really upsetting you a lot. If someone goes ahead and tries or says something that really does anger you and you go right ahead and ignore your own feelings, then that means that you are also ignoring the trigger as well. In other words, if something is imperative enough to you that it is capable of causing a lot of emotional distress, then it is obviously far too significant to be outrightly dismissed as such.

o   Always learn to control your reactions

A friend might say something very hurtful or a romantic partner might seem particularly distant or your child might be cranky. The odds are that any and all of these things can easily spark a negative reaction that can drive you to say something potentially damaging and negative. When you are very angry, you might say stuff that you would not do so in normal circumstances. On the other hand, it might seem as if it is not possible to control your emotions at that point in time, but if you really work at it, yes, you can actually manage to control your reaction via certain intrinsic triggers that are entirely under your control.

In a nutshell, by learning to control any and all of your otherwise hotheaded and impulsive responses, you can also pause to reflect and re-consider the situation, thereby speaking or acting in certain ways that will always best serve you.

o   What if your childhood is still making you angry?

If you were always hurt and abused as a child, then there is a high chance that you are still carrying all that repressed anger inside you. This means that if your teachers, elder siblings and parents were harsh and used unkind words to scold you, then you will also end up doing exactly the same in a bid to get rid of all that repressed anger and rage that has been welling inside. If you were often called "stupid" and "lazy", then you might have developed a hatred for these words and by using them on others, you might try to eliminate that hate and feel at peace with yourself. Unfortunately, using such negative words in any capacity towards people who look up to you would end up making them feel really bad, thereby perpetuating the same vicious cycle. Today, as an adult (for instance), whenever your boss will ask you to effectively redo a report that has any sort of errors, you will automatically respond with a lot of anger, but whatever triggered such a reaction has a whole lot more to do with your own past than the words coming out of your boss's mouth.

- o Reactivity can both effectively quietly destroy otherwise strong relationships

Whenever you try to talk it out with your spouse or common-law partner, wheneither of you is feeling really reactive, then it is pertinent to note that nothing will ever be gained by just a talk. Here, you are not talking to get your point across, instead you are trying to 'hammer' it across so that you 'win' the argument. There is no listening here at all. You will only end up saying more hurtful things in a bizarre game of one up-man-ship. In the end, both of you will lose, chiefly because no one is interested in listening at all. This kind of negative reaction can easily lead to a really toxic relationship, where one or even both of you will walk on the proverbial eggshells in fear of causing the kind of fight that will only make matters worse, while the underlying problems that led to the heated exchange are never even revealed or dealt with.

- o Being self-aware and mindful is the diametrical opposite of reactivity

Here it is important to understand that some really good relationships do not just happen entirely by accident. This is because you have both worked on them in your own way. As a matter of fact, anger that is handled in an otherwise unhealthy manner will keep youand all those people that you love from getting exactlywhat you need or want from life, as well as from each other as well. It is important to understand that such mindfulness is the supreme key to unlocking certain reallyhealthy reactions to various triggers and latent anger, chiefly because mindfulness is the absolute opposite of reactivity.

- o How to Move Forward

If you really want to know how you can pause and reflect before you speak or lash out in anger, then the very first step to change the way you interact with others is to identify different problems and to accept overall responsibility for the same. Just try and look at yourself honestly and candidly, and also do a reallymindful review of the role that your anger has basicallyplayed in all of your relationships. Only then can you begin the whole process of learning how to try, access and ultimately process your core feelings. Once you commit yourself to changing the way you always think and behave, you can take back the power over your whole life. By using mindfulness to repair the wounds caused by negative words, you can try and move forward in the spirit of forgiveness and gratitude.

Positive language at work

In the workplace the seminal importance of positive language can never really be overstressed. As a matter of fact, should you be able to effortlessly communicate more positively, then it is all the more likely that you will be able to elicit a modicum of cooperation rather than indulging in useless arguments and confrontation that are no help to anyone. This holds true irrespective of the fact that you are communicating with clients or customers, your staff and employees, government workers or just about anyone else that you might be liable to encounter in the workplace. In any case you can easily use reallypositive language toproject both inwards and outwards a really helpful as well as positive image, rather than opting for a destructive negative one.

o The ubiquitous 'Naysayer'

No doubt just about everyone is quite familiar with the ubiquitous "Naysayer". In a nutshell this is a person who enthusiastically plays the role of 'devil's advocate' and more often than not, offers criticism of ideas. Such a person, rarely if ever offers good suggestions or workable alternatives, but nonethelessis really good at gleefully picking holes in the ideas of otherhard-working people.

For those unfortunate people who have actually worked with just such a colleague, they have a pretty good idea as to the kind of negativity such communication brings alongside it. Not only is it really tiring for those individuals who are often forced by circumstances to be around just such a person, but apart from that, the near constant strain of havingall their ideas challenged by the naysayer, creates a very negative environment, and also significantly increases confrontation as well.

Here, it is pertinent to note that the naysayer does not always bringa markedlynegative attitude to the table. On the contrary, he or she will simply use language that effectively gives an impression of the core negativity, behind any statement. In a nutshell, these people have just simply not learned to phrase their individualcomments in somewhat more constructive and positive ways.

It is all too easy to fall into any sort ofnegative language pattern. In fact, quite a few of us do so without ever even being aware of it, not just verbally but also in written communication as well. Let us take a closer look at the following arch-typical government memo.

o Example one

"We regret to inform you that we will not be able process your application since you have neglected to provide us the required information."

While it is quite polite (in spite of the fact that it is certainly overly formal), it is also quite negative as well. Consider the fact that it also includes multiple negative words and phrases such as 'will not' andneglected. Ultimately the actual tone also suggests that the recipient of this missive is the one to blame for the problem at hand.

o How positive words can help here

Let us contrast the above example with a different, re-written but more positive approach towards the same issue.

o Example two

"Congratulations on setting up your new business. In order to register your business name, it is vital that we get some additional information. If you were to return the enclosed form, with all of the highlighted areas duly filled in, we will certainly be able to send you your own business registration certificate within a fortnight, at most.

If we were to juxtapose these two memos together we will be able to note that the first negative example will tell the recipient that he or

27

she is at fault. Moreover, it does not stress the comparatively more positive things that should be donein order tobasically remedy this issue, on a suitably permanent basis, once and for all. It is not that the relevant information is not present there in the first example. All the information is there in that short memo. Howeverit sounds quite bureaucratic, cold and downright negative. On the other hand, the comparatively more positive example sounds totallydifferent, even though it contains near identical information. Basically, it is a tad more "upbeat" and also helpful as well.

Different types of Negative & Positive words and Phrases in the workplace

Most common negative phrasing and language tend to have the following characteristics:

- Negative terminology and its impact

- They will inform the recipient what cannot be done, rather than emphasizing what can actuallybe achieved
- They bear subtle blame game undertones
- Includes words like won't, can't, unable to, in order to inform the former recipient what the sender cannot do, rather than what he actually can accomplish
- It does not stress any sort of positive actions or for that matter, even otherwise positive consequences

o   Positive words and phrases and how they work

On the other hand, different types of positive phrasing, words, and language have the following characteristics:

- o They inform the recipient what can be done, rather than emphasizing on what cannot be done
- o They also suggest various healthy alternatives and choices that are available to the recipient of the message
- o They sound quite helpful and encouraging rather than seeming to be bureaucratic
- o They also stress various highly positive actions and also offer positive consequences that can easily be anticipated

o   Some of the more common negative language, words and phrases

If you really intend to move towards a more positive form of communication at the workplace, then the first task will be to first and foremost identify and eliminate the different types of common negative phrases that we are prone to use in the workplace. The following examples are not only quite commonbut at the same time they should be avoided whenever it is possible for you to do so, easily enough:

- o Various expressions that tend to suggest a degree of carelessness
- o You overlooked the attached or the enclosing...
- o You failed to include...

- o   You neglected to specify...

- o   Different phrases that appear to suggest that the recipient is lying
- o   You claim that...
- o   You state that...
- o   You say that...

- o   Any expressions that seem to cast aspersions on the recipient's intelligence
- o   I fail to understand...
- o   We utterly cannot see how you...
- o   We are at a total loss to understand...

- o   Different types of highly demanding phrases that tend to imply coercion or pressure
- o   You ought to...
- o   You should...
- o   We must ask you to...
- o   You must...
- o   We must insist...
- o   You absolutely have to...

- o   Various phrases that might easily be interpreted as being unduly sarcastic or patronizing
- o   We will thank you to...
- o   No doubt...
- o   You understand, of course...
- o   Please respond soon...
- o   You will doubtless...

- Are you sure you can?
- Do you think it is possible for you to…?

- Learning how to utilize positive phrases

If you are ever going to successfully eliminate negative phrases from your professional and personal life, then it is imperative that you replace them with more positive forms of expression that convey much the same information, albeit in a more positive context. Let us sift through a few examples of such positive phrasing and terminology.

- If you can send us [any kind of information related to the subject matter at hand], we can easily complete the process for you
- The information that we currently have,basically suggests that your viewpoint on this issue is different from ours. Kindly Let us explain our perspective
- Might we try and suggest that you [insert suggestion here]
- There is an option open to you [insert option here]
- We can also help you to [whatever may be required] if you can send us [whatever may be needed]

- Informal exercise

Once you have understood the slight differences in terms of context and diction in the above examples, it is suggested that you should take a suitably quick look at a few memos that you might have written. Now go through each and every one of them word by word and highlight the sentences that you feel have an overtly negative tone.

Now that you have been alerted to the subtler aspects of your own self written memos that send demeaning or bureaucraticmessages, you can then rewrite them all over again. Then juxtapose the older ones with the ones you have written now and then compare the difference between the two.

Ultimately, just about all sorts of negative language effectively conveys a markedly poor image to not just clients and customers alike but also to all those people around us that have a direct impact on our professional lives (such as colleagues and subordinates, for instance). Sometimes such negative terminology ends up causing conflict and confrontation, which is neither necessary nordesired. This is why the first place to start using any sort of positive language is in written material. Once the art of writing positively has been properly developed, it will be considerably easier to change your spoken language in order to present a far more positive tone.

Speaking positively at work: Making a game plan that actually works

Many people tend to harbor a habit of repeating the same negative phrases and words over and over again. Here the core problem is that the more we read, hear, or speak a phrase, the more power it will have over us. This is largely due to the fact that the human brain often uses constant repetition in order to learn more.

However, the really good news is that it is entirely possible to break this seemingly noxious habit once and for all. In the long run, this means that it is quite possible to change negative language by infusing it with markedly positive undertones. And of course, doing this will not only make you sound a whole lot more confident, but others will also see you in the same light.

But it is important that you focus and work hard in order to achieve your goal. Especially, in light of the fact that the results will definitely be worth it. Many experts believe that It can take as much as three weeks or so to break out of the rut of negative speech. This is why you should have a well thought out game plan already at hand before you attempt to do the needful.

o Changing your habits

First things first, in order to change your habits, it is very important that you should start to identify the negative phrases or words that you tend to use on adaily basis. And one of the simplest way to check if you are using negative terms and phrases is to try and listen to yourself. Even if this may sound like a really easy thing to do, it does require an element of self-discipline. And it is not something that we tend to do naturally. After all, we have been trained from early childhood to focus on what others are saying to usrather than what we are saying ourselves.

Once you have become conscious of whether you are using positive or negative language, especially when talking in any environment where other peoples' perception of you really matters, you will be able to exercise a measure of restraint with regard to negative speech.

Let us study the following phase *"Does that even make sense?"*

Now this is a good example of a really negative sentence that can potentially give someone a really bad first impression.

After all, why say something that not only sounds quite derisive but also completely unnecessary. Furthermore, it also makes you sound almost as if you doubt yourself. As a matter of fact, when you ask this entirely pointless and rhetorical question, your listener/s might start to wonder whether 'you' are actually making any sense. Moreover, this will immediately make them feel defensive about their opinion and they will then try and defend it, ultimately igniting a never-ending argument.

Yes, it is possible that you may have the best of intentions and may have inadvertently said this phase in order to encourage more interaction. However, what you are actually doing is basically sowing the seed of doubt quite unnecessarily. And as a corollary to that, you are also directly questioning your own ability to speak at length on the subject matter in question.

So, the very next time that you might be interested in checking to see if your listener really understands you, instead of using the interrogatory sentence "does that make sense", you can say something along the lines of "do you have any thoughts or questions on the [subject matter]?"

By using positive or even neutral language, you will be in a position to give your target audience a great opportunity to ask something they do not understand without being humiliated. At the same time, you will also be able to convey the important message that you are very confident about the subject. And since confidence begets confidence, you will actually start to 'feel' that you are in fact the 'go to' expert on the topic.

So, the very next time you are interested in knowing if someone really understands you, then instead of using such negative phrases that cast doubts on your listeners' abilities, you can substitute them with more positive sounding questions that enable them to express themselves.

o "I'm sorry..."

It is pretty common to hear people stating that they are profoundly sorry, even when an apology is not really necessary at all. The usual practice is that they tend to prefix sentences with an apologetic tone such as "Sorry, would you mind if I sit at this table?" ... "Sorry, can you tell me the time please" ... Some people even apologize for asking for information, "Sorry, could I ask a question?"

Saying sorry like it's some sort of mantra, even when it is not even remotely warranted, simply makes an unashamedly apologetic person look as though he or she is singularly lacking confidence. After all, if you are constantly communicating an outrightly submissive message to people all the time, then they will hardly be interested at looking at you as a peer. This can make a huge difference in a work environment. Here, the very last thing you need is to be doubted when you are trying to explain your position.

You should always be particularly careful of being a 'serial sorry sayer.' You can always try replacing the apologetic 'sorry' with the more neutral 'excuse me,'since this is what you really meant.

o If only..."

If you have developed a near constant habit of saying this, then it is important that you strike it out of your vocabulary. The only thing this phase communicates is negativity.

"If only I was more fit", "If only we had more time to spend together," "If only I was a wealthier person", "If only it wasnot raining." This list is practically endless, and the more you use this phrase, the more people will get frustrated with you.

Ultimately, muttering "if only" is an entirely pointless exercise. This phrase is not only utterly incapable of solving any problems, but it also conveys the distinct impression that you have given up already.

However, if you are more focused on thinking more positively, it will be quite easy to remove "if only" from your vocabulary, altogether. This is why negative and pessimistic people generally struggle the most with this habit. Furthermore, it is always better to accept reality rather than going "if only... I was a more positive person."

It is pertinent to note that highly positive people who have loads of charismaand look and sound really confident do not ever use such kind of negative language. There is a fairly simple reason for this. The two just simply do not go together. Sometimes, in interviews or really grueling and difficult work meetings, such negative terminology tends to slip in during long discussions, and this is why you should always be on guard when participating in important discussions.

Always remember that these seemingly small and subtle language changes can go on to make a really huge difference to other people's perception of your professionalism, as well as overall confidence.Once you have managed to acquire a really high degree of mental awareness of your own use of negative phrases and words, then it means that now it is entirely possible for you to control exactly how confident and positive you should sound in both your written memos and letters as well as your speech.

Using the Tremendous Power of Positive Language at Home

Positive words and phrases are as important at home as they are at the workplace. This is due to the fact that your family is your primary relationship, and the words that you use to communicate with your spouse, siblings, parents and most important of all, your children have a direct bearing on all other relationships.

When you use positive terminology to convey your ideas and instructions, it will bring forth an immediate and positive reaction from the people around you. Let us look at it in a parent to child perspective:

o Children Are Automatically Empowered When They Listen to Positive Language

When any parent (or guardian) of a child switches from negative language (such as "Stop," "No," "Don't") to highly positive language, then they will quickly realize that there will be lesswhining and tantrums from their offspring. While this may seem like a slight change, it can still make a world of difference for your child and in your own dealings with the people around you. Here is how positive language can make a crucial difference:

o Positive Language Will Tell a Child What They Can Do Rather Than What They Can't Do at All

For many children,orders and commands regarding what they cannot do may turn out to be quite counterproductive. This is due to the fact that they tend to have a hard time understanding what they 'can' do.

o Example

Ms. Smith while admonishing John, her son, says, "Do not climb the bookcase." In this case, little John may seem to be quite conflicted as he has no idea what he 'should' be doing in the meantime. However, if she were to say "John, you need to keep your feet on the floor," he will understand exactly what he needs to do, i.e., not go around climbing stuff.

In other words, using such highly positive language will considerably increase the overall chances that your child will do exactly what 'you' want, and furthermore, it will also have a truly wonderful effect on the overall tone of the whole day. After all, if you always constantly feel that you are being negative by saying "Stop doing that," Do not do this," then you will, as a parent, eventually start feeling really discouraged. This is why positive language is such a big part of good parenting. And as such it must be encouraged till it becomes part and parcel of your everyday life. Let us see how you can do that:

- o Step 1: Identify all The Negative Terms and Language That You Constantly Use at Home

Self-awareness is the most important part of reducing negative language at home. This means that you will have to be totally aware of any negative words, phrases and language that you are constantly using all the time so that you can correct yourself.

For instance, is there any sort of behavior thatconsistently makes you react in a highly negative way? Doesyour child start screaming at the top of his or her lungs every time you shout "Stop"?

You will have to think long and hard about what it is that triggers such behavior and compels you to use negative language in front of people that you love and care about. Yes, such identification may not come easily, but once you become self-aware with regard to your own negativity, then it will be a burden you will be able to shed with a certain measure of relief.

- Step 2: Learn Some Positive Phases as an Alternative to the Negative Ones and Start Using Them

With the passage of time, you will pick up various highly positive phrases that you will use for certain situations. There will come a time when such positive phrases will become second nature to you whenever you want someone to do something for you. Here it is pertinent to understand that there is no specific swap for the word "no", especially when it comes to children. In fact, you will have to come up with positive phases on the spot subject to the situation at hand. However, it is always important to treat the little ones with the same respect that you would bestow on your peers, regardless of the specific situation that you are addressing. Consider the following examples and how they can be turned around from being negative to positive:

- Stop running: Slow down
- Don't hit your brother: Be gentle when you touch your brother
- Stop yelling: Quiet voice please
- Don't throw the ball around: Put the ball on the ground or keep it in your hands
- Don't cry: I can see you are very upset, and I am there for you if you want to talk about it

Always remember that speaking positively will not only have a major effect on the emotional and mental wellbeing of your child, but it will also be good for you. And you will start radiating your own aura of positivity that will infect everyone close to you in its warm, soothing light.

- Step 3: Always Set the Appropriate Boundaries

Being positive certainly does not mean that you will not set the right boundaries, that you are too soft, and that others can get away with anything and everything. As a matter of fact, once your children acquire a clear idea of what is ok and what is not, then it will be much easier for them to understand you. Hence, they will end up doing whatever is expected of them. In the long run, this means you will not have to spend so much time correcting them.

Ultimately, such appropriate boundaries will also help to empower your child/children. They will be inspired enough to always do the right thing and in time, this will actively decrease their overall need for near constant correction.

o   Step 4: Evolve Your Positive Language Out of Spoken
     Commands

Once you successfully start using positive language at home, you have to evolve your linguistic skills in such a manner that you will no longer need to seek recourse to literal commands at all. Always remember that kids may have to listen to commands all day, but is this how we, as adults, really talk to each other? Of course not. We try to reason it out or make requests to our fellow peers. For example, you can ask an adult for a favor and say, "Can you please turn the volume down, I find it really hard to concentrate," and they will do the needful. You can do the same with children as well. This is a pretty nifty tool indeed, because it will teach kids to be reasonable. And they will realize that you are getting bothered by their racket, and they will turn it down the volume a bit.

Conclusion

In the light of the above, we can safely conclude that irrespective of the home or workplace, the amazing power of positive language and words can easily create a whole new world of positivity all around you. And since positive words lead to positive thoughts and actions, pretty soon you will find yourself surrounded with equally positive people, who have all gotten this far because of you and your positive language and attitude.

"If we understood the power of our thoughts, we would guard them more closely. If we understood the awesome power of our words, we would prefer silence to almost anything negative. In our thoughts and words, we create our own weaknesses and our own strengths. Our limitations and joys begin in our hearts. We can always replace negative with positive."

Betty Eadie

Printed in Great Britain
by Amazon